A PILGRIM'S
PRAYERS

A PILGRIM'S
PRAYERS

*I hope the prayers
in this little book
will encourage you
in your walk with the Lord.*

Douglas Wyant

DOUGLAS WYANT

 COURIER PUBLISHING

Greenville, South Carolina

A Pilgrim's Prayers
Copyright © 2021 Douglas Wyant
All Rights Reserved

ISBN 978-1-955295-00-0

Library of Congress Control Number: 2021910449
REL087000: Religion/Prayer
POE000000: Poetry/General
POE003000: Poetry/Subjects & Themes/Inspirational & Religious

A Pilgrim's Prayers is available for order from most bookstores and
online booksellers. To order in bulk (10 or more copies), contact
Courier Publishing, 100 Manly St., Greenville, SC, 29601, 864-232-
8736, for quantity pricing.

COURIER PUBLISHING
GREENVILLE, SOUTH CAROLINA

DEDICATION

With gratitude to Jesus Christ,
who urges us to ask.

TABLE OF CONTENTS

Prologue

Sunday evening, January 28, 2018, a CT scan in the Kershaw Health Emergency Room revealed a mass in my colon.

Throughout my journey with cancer, I watched for signs of encouragement. In February, on my first trip to Durham, North Carolina, for a consultation with the chief colorectal surgeon at Duke University Hospital, I noticed a billboard on I-95 that declared, "Everything is possible if you only believe."

On March 12, the surgeon at Duke removed my ascending colon and twenty-three lymph nodes. Four of them tested positive.

Some people choose a word to focus on each year. In January 2018, the editor of *Journey*, "A Woman's Guide to Intimacy with God," chose *trust*. She said, "I continue to believe and trust in the reliability of Scripture and in the character of God. If things always went according to our plan, we would never have any opportunities to need or trust God … ."

I'd received a brown, leather-bound journal with

"TRUST" and "Blessed is the man who trusts in the LORD" embossed on the front cover as a Christmas gift in 2017. So, even before I realized I had colon cancer, I'd decided *trust* would be my word for 2018. During the six months I kept a record of my spiritual journey in this journal, from January first through June twenty-third, *trust* or a variant (*trusts, trusted, trusting, trustworthy,* or *entrust*) appeared 282 times.

Many of the prayer-poems in *A Pilgrim's Prayers* were written in response to Scripture that came to my attention primarily through daily devotions while I recuperated from surgery and chemotherapy. In 2019, using the poetry in the Psalms as a model, I began to convert my 2018 prayers in prose into free verse.

Most of the prayers in this book are brief. When we're desperate, our prayers are often short. Terrified when he began to sink as he walked on the Sea of Galilee toward Jesus during a storm, Peter cried out, "Lord, save me!" (Matthew 14:30, NIV). In the temple in Jerusalem, a repentant tax collector pleaded, "God, have mercy on me, a sinner" (Luke

18:13, NIV). From the cross, Jesus cried out in a loud voice, "My God, my God, why have you forsaken me?" (Matthew 27:46, NIV).

Jesus told his disciples, "You are the light of the world" (Matthew 5:14, NIV). Like Job — who continued to trust in God after losing his children, his wealth, and his health — we shine brightest on dark days, so we shouldn't be surprised when God places us in difficult circumstances.

Prayer is a dialogue, not a monologue. God speaks to me through his Word; then I respond to him in prayer. I believe my prayers are more effective when they're rooted in God's Word.

Writing out my prayers is a daily discipline for me. I'm easily distracted, so writing helps me stay focused. Although I pray short, silent prayers throughout the day, I prefer to write out my prayers in longhand at the kitchen table after breakfast.

I begin many of my prayers with gratitude. The apostle Paul instructs us not only to "give thanks in all circumstances" (1 Thessalonians 5:18, NIV), but also to "give thanks for everything to God the Father in the name of our Lord Jesus Christ" (Ephesians 5:20, NLT), because "we know that God causes everything to work together for the good of those who love God" (Romans 8:28, NLT).

Joseph, who forgave his brothers who'd sold him into slavery when he was seventeen, is proof that Romans 8:28 is true. Years later, when he was in a position of authority in Egypt, second only to Pharaoh, Joseph told his brothers, "You intended to harm me, but God intended it all for good. He brought me to this position so I could save the lives of many people" (Genesis 50:20, NLT). But the ultimate proof of the veracity of Romans 8:28 is the crucifixion of Christ, whose sacrificial death has saved the lives of multitudes. Therefore, we call the day he suffered for our sins Good Friday.

Salvation — accepting Jesus Christ as our Savior — is a once-in-a-lifetime event: "If you confess with your mouth that Jesus is Lord and believe in your heart that God raised him from the dead, you will be saved" (Romans 10:9, NLT). But sanctification — becoming like Jesus, which is God's purpose for us

(Romans 8:28-29) — is a lifelong process that won't be complete until we see him (1 John 3:2). "And I am certain that God, who began the good work within you, will continue his work until it is finally finished on the day when Christ Jesus returns" (Philippians 1:6, NLT).

Thank you, LORD, for creating each of us in your image. Thank you for loving us so much you sent your Son to die for us, so that we might live with you forever. Thank you for our troubles, which compel us to cry out to you. Thank you for being merciful and gracious to us. Thank you for forgiving and for forgetting all our sins. Thank you for protecting us from our enemies, visible and invisible. Thank you for providing everything we need. Thank you for responding to our prayers with compassion and wisdom. Thank you, Father, for working in each of our lives in unique ways to draw us closer to you and make us more like your Son, Jesus Christ, with whom you were always well pleased.

A PILGRIM'S
PRAYERS

Marching Orders

The LORD said to me,
You've stayed here long enough.
It's time to move on …
Don't be afraid —
I will go ahead of you,
and I will fight for you.

A Declaration of Dependence

Lord, I acknowledge
>my dependence on you.
If you didn't exist,
>I wouldn't exist.
Without you
>I couldn't take another breath
>or write another word.

The Sin of Silence

Jesus, you commissioned us
    to be your witnesses,
but I'm ashamed to admit
    I've never told anyone
    what you've done for me.

Good Friday

Although it's easy to blame the Jews,
  who clamored for your crucifixion,
or the Roman soldiers, who flogged you
  and nailed you to the cross,
Scripture asserts you died for my sins, too.

Jesus, I'm one of those for whom you prayed,
  Father, forgive ...

BLESSED ASSURANCE

Thank you, LORD, for the assurance
    you're always with me —
    no matter where I am
    or what I'm going through.
Thank you, LORD, for holding my hand.

FAMILY OF FAITH

Thank you, Father, for choosing me
    to be one of your children.
Thank you for adopting me
    into your family of faith.
Thank you for demonstrating
    your love for me
    by disciplining me.
Thank you, Father, for the prayers
    of my spiritual siblings.

Blessed Trinity

Lord God Almighty —

    Father, Son, and Holy Spirit,

    creator and sustainer of the universe,

    savior and sanctifier of our souls —

I praise you for who you are;

I thank you for what you've done for us.

PRECIOUS PROMISES

The LORD who created me says,
    I am the LORD your God.
You're precious to me — I love you.
I've ransomed you — you are mine.
Don't be afraid — I am with you.

Day by day, I sustain you.
I protect you, and I provide
    everything you need.
I will never abandon you.
Not even death can separate us —
    I promise.

Standing on the Promises of God

Thank you, Lord, for my problems,
which compel me to cry out to you.

Almighty God, my life is in your hands.
Shield me from my invisible enemies.

Lord, I'm neither anxious nor afraid
because my faith is rooted in your Word.

I Believe

Lord, my faith is anchored
in your inerrant, infallible Word.
Like Peter, I believe
you are the Christ,
the Son of the living God.
Like Martha, I believe
you have the power to raise the dead.
Like David, I believe
I will dwell in your house forever.

I Witness

Lord, fill my heart with your love,
    my mind with your wisdom,
    my mouth with your words.

Empower me to share your message
    of love and mercy and grace
    joyfully and generously,
    with compassion and courage.

Please Pray for Me

Father, on dismal days —
when I'm too depressed
or discouraged to pray —
I'm grateful
your Son and your Spirit
intercede for me.

FORGIVEN

Thank you, LORD, for forgiving me —
not only for the bad things I've done,
but also for the good things I haven't done.

REVELATIONS

Thank you, LORD, for your Word,
    inspired by your Holy Spirit,
which not only reveals who you are
    and what you've done for us,
but also tells us who we are,
    why we're here,
    and where we're going.

GUILTY AS CHARGED

LORD, I confess I don't love you
    with all my heart,
    all my soul,
    and all my mind.

I admit I'm deliberately disobedient,
    rebellious and devious,
    selfish and stubborn.

I often act as if you don't exist —
    as if there is no reward for the righteous
    and no punishment for the wicked.

Remember This

My wife says I've got a selective memory —
I remember only what I want to remember,
    not what she expects me to remember.

Lord, I'm glad you have a selective memory, too.
You promise to forgive and forget all my sins,
    but you declare, I will not forget you!

LION ON A LEASH

Sovereign LORD, your Word reveals
    Satan's power is restricted —
    he can't do anything
    without your permission.

LORD, I ask you to thwart the plans
    of my ancient adversary,
    the prince of this world,
    who prowls around in the dark,
    roaring like a ravenous lion.
May he fall into the pit he has dug for me.

LESSON LEARNED

I've learned that the more I complain,
the more I have to complain about,
but the more I thank you, LORD,
the more you give me to be thankful for.

Thank You, Father

Thank you for life — abundant and eternal.

Thank you for your unfailing, everlasting love.

Thank you for being merciful and gracious to me.

Thank you for the gifts of your Son and your Spirit.

Thank you for giving me reasons to rejoice every day.

You Know

Lord, you know me —
    you know everything about me.
You know how weak and wicked I am,
    and yet, you love me
    with an unfathomable love.

HOUND OF HEAVEN

Thank you, LORD, for your relentless love.
May you be as patient and persistent
    in your pursuit
      of my errant family and friends
      as you have been with me.

O GOD!

When I whimper, when I wail,
when I howl in impotent rage,
    my prayers are reduced
    to two words,
    repeated like a refrain —
O God!

LIFE PRESERVER

Pain wakes me before dawn.
On my knees in the throne room,
    I cry out to you, LORD —
    my invincible fortress
    my refuge in trouble
    the ark of my salvation
    and my soul's sanctuary.

LORD, remember your promises.
Please answer me quickly.
Preserve my life so I may praise you.

Solo Deo

According to your Word, Lord,
      before our first ancestors
      ate the forbidden fruit,
      you'd paid the penalty
      for their disobedience.

Of all the gods we bow down to,
      only you loved us so much
      you'd rather die
      than live without us.

Lord, you alone are worthy of worship.

My Plea

O Lord,
hear me
help me
heal me.

A REPENTANT SINNER

Release me, LORD,
from Satan's snares.

O LORD, cleanse me.
Purge me. Purify me.
Blot out all my sins.

And may many who see
what you've done for me
fear and trust you, too.

RESCUE ME

O LORD, I cry out to you
from the depths of despair.

Have mercy on me, LORD.
Have mercy on me.

Lift me out of this dark pit,
set my feet on solid ground,
and steady me, LORD,
as we walk along together.

My Helper

Some people say God helps
      those who help themselves.
But Scripture teaches us God helps
      those who have enough faith
      and humility to ask for help.

My help comes from you, LORD,
      my Maker and my Master.

Promise Keeper

Lord, I exalt you
for your faithfulness.
I praise you, Lord,
because you always
keep your promises.

AN APPEAL FOR DELIVERANCE

I beseech you, LORD, to save me
from my most aggressive enemy,
    my most formidable foe.
LORD God, save me from myself.

UNCONDITIONAL SURRENDER

Okay, LORD, I give up.
Hands above my head,
I surrender unconditionally.
I'm your servant, LORD.
Where am I needed most?

AND THE BLIND SHALL SEE

Sovereign LORD, help me see
    my circumstances
    from your perspective.
Help me look beyond
    my present pain
    to the joy awaiting me.

HONOR DUE

Father, thank you for my father
> and my mother —
> who loved me
> nurtured me
> protected me
> provided for me
> and disciplined me,
> as they emulated you.

CELEBRATE FREEDOM

Thank you, Father, for our country
and for the freedoms we enjoy here —
especially the freedom to worship you.

Thank you for the men and women
who dedicated their lives
to attain and maintain our freedom.

Most of all, thank you for Jesus,
whose sacrificial death on the cross
secured our spiritual freedom.

PRINCE OF PEACE

Thank you, Jesus,
for the promise of peace.

In this tumultuous world,
only your presence
makes peace possible.

MORNING JOY

Good morning, LORD.
Thank you for this day —
a day unlike any other day
    you've ever made.
What do you want me to do
    for you today?

Evening Rest

After a difficult day at work,
I thank you, Lord,
for a quiet evening at home.

A CHRISTIAN'S CREED

Christ Jesus, I believe you, who created everything
     in heaven and on earth,
     were conceived by the power of the Holy Spirit.
I believe you were born of a virgin, as the Bread of Life,
     in Bethlehem, the house of bread.
I believe you healed the sick, raised the dead,
     and prepared the disciples to become apostles.
I believe you were crucified for our sins,
     even though you were innocent of any offense.
I believe you rose to life again
     three days after your burial in a borrowed tomb.
I believe you were seen by over five hundred believers
     before you ascended into heaven.
I believe you are seated at the right hand of our Father,
     constantly interceding for us.
I believe you will return soon to collect your saints,
     defeat that old dragon, the devil, and his minions,
     and judge us based on our response to your sacrifice.
I believe those whose names are written in the book of life,
     those whose transgressions your blood blotted out,
     shall sing your praises throughout eternity.

I Love You, I Love You Not

I love you, LORD —

> my source
>
> my shield
>
> my shelter
>
> my savior
>
> my strength
>
> my helper
>
> my healer
>
> my hope
>
> my delight
>
> my reward.

LORD, help me learn to love

> my obnoxious neighbor.

Help Wanted

Thank you, LORD, for the assurance
      your grace is sufficient
      for me in any situation.

Please give me a double portion
      of your grace today.

FINISHER OF OUR FAITH

Thank you, LORD, for the good work
    you've begun in me.
Unlike me, you always finish
    what you start.

EFFECTIVE PRAYERS

LORD, although I'm not blameless,
     you consider me righteous
     because of my faith in you.
So, I enter your holy presence boldly,
     confident you will respond
     with compassion and wisdom
     to my earnest, fervent prayers.

THE GIFT OF CANCER

Like Paul, I accept a thorn in the flesh
     as a gift from you, LORD —
a constant reminder of our need for your grace.
And our only appropriate response is gratitude.

My Creator and My Redeemer

The LORD said to me, I am your God.
I created you —
in my own image I created you.

Before you became a slave to sin,
I redeemed you —
with my own blood I redeemed you.

PRAYER WARRIOR

LORD, I'm on guard —
    waiting,
    watching,
    working for you —
armed with the sword of the Spirit,
praying for a bountiful harvest.

A Mind in Turmoil

Why are you my adversary, Lord?
Why do you laugh at my schemes,
    defer my dreams,
    and foil my plans?

Why do you refuse to respond
    to my urgent requests?
Have I exhausted your patience?
Is there no more mercy for me?

Solace in Scripture

When I'm distraught, Lord,
    your Word is a balm
    for my anxious heart.

Thank You, Jesus

Despised and rejected,
you suffered for us —
pierced for our transgressions
crushed for our iniquities
punished for our sins —
so that we will not perish
but inherit everlasting life.

Pro Bono

Christ Jesus, please take my case.
As my advocate, defend me
  against vicious attacks
  by malicious witnesses.
Defeat my treacherous enemies.
Plead for my acquittal,
and deliver me from perdition.

Lord, I have nothing to offer you
as compensation for your service
except my profuse gratitude —
Thank you, Jesus. Thank you.

To Do

I'm still struggling, LORD,

> to resist temptation
>
> to love my enemies
>
> to forgive those who sin against me
>
> to be content in any situation
>
> to pray continually
>
> to be joyful in adversity
>
> to thank you for everything.

So, I'm glad my salvation doesn't depend

> on my good works.

MY WEAKNESS, YOUR STRENGTH

O LORD, I need you.
Without you
I can't do anything.
But with you
anything is possible.

I need your help, LORD.
Don't deny my appeal.
Answer my urgent cry.
Be merciful to me.
Show me your favor.

A PRAYER FOR A SICK FRIEND

My friend is suffering —
    his body is weak;
    his faith is feeble.
LORD God, comfort him.
Make him aware of your
presence and your power
your mercy and your grace
and your immeasurable love.

Lord, Why Am I Suffering?

The Sovereign Lord said to me, I am holy,
and I expect you to be holy, too; therefore,
I must refine you in the furnace of affliction.

Don't be afraid. Don't be discouraged.
You're not alone. I am with you.
I will neither fail you nor forsake you.
I will strengthen you, and I will help you.

MORNING, NOON, AND NIGHT

When troubles overwhelm me,
I bring my burdens to you, LORD,
trusting you to liberate me again.

TOTAL COMMITMENT

LORD, may I be spiritually sensitive
to the guidance of your Holy Spirit.
Show me what you want me to do,
and give me the faith and the courage
necessary to obey you immediately,
regardless of the consequences.

Unspoken

I often feel
inadequate
insignificant
incompetent
inarticulate,
and yet, Lord,
you chose me.

Only with you,
precious Jesus,
can I be candid,
without fear
of condemnation.

To Be

Holy Spirit, help me
Be holy.
Be kind.
Be good.
Be joyful.
Be gentle.
Be patient.
Be fruitful.
Be faithful.
Be hopeful.
Be merciful.
Be gracious.
Be thankful.
Be peaceful.
Be obedient.
Be generous.
Be persistent.
Be courageous.
Be compassionate.
Be self-disciplined.

EVENING STAR

LORD, I've relied on you all my life.
You're the shepherd of my soul
    my constant companion
    generous provider
    faithful guide
    vigilant guard
    compassionate caregiver
    the source of my strength
    and the secret of my success.

May I continue to flourish in old age.
At 85, may I be as vigorous as Caleb.
LORD, may my last years on earth
be the most productive years of my life.

An Act of Faith

I believe; therefore, I pray.

Lord, enable me to pray
frequently and fervently,
persistently and expectantly,
as long as you give me breath.

Scripture Sources

All of these prayer-poems were inspired by Scripture. Unless otherwise indicated, all Scripture sources are from the New International Version (NIV) of the Bible. Other Scripture sources are the New Living Translation (NLT), the New King James Version (NKJV), and *The Message* (MSG).

The number preceding each title below matches the page number of the prayer-poem in the text.

v   Dedication: Matthew 7:7-8; John 14:13-14; 15:7, 16; 16:23-24.

19   Marching Orders: Deuteronomy 1:6-7a, NLT; 29-30, NLT.

20   A Declaration of Dependence: Hebrews 11:6; John 15:5.

21   The Sin of Silence: Matthew 28:18-20; Acts 1:8;
      Mark 5:1-20; James 4:17.

22   Good Friday: Matthew 27:1-54; Mark 15:1-39; Luke
      22:66-23:47; John 18:12-19:37; Romans 5:8;
      1 Corinthians 15:3; 1 John 1:9.

23   Blessed Assurance: Deuteronomy 31:6, 8; Joshua
      1:5, 9; Isaiah 41:10; 43:2, 5a.

24   Family of Faith: John 1:12; Ephesians 1:4-5, NLT;
      6:18, NLT; Hebrews 12:6, 8, NLT.

25   Blessed Trinity: Genesis 1:1; John 1:1-3; 3:16;
      Colossians 1:15-17; Acts 16:31; Romans 10:9, 13;
      Joel 2:32; 2 Thessalonians 2:13.

26   Precious Promises: Isaiah 43:1-5, NLT; Romans
      8:32-39; 2 Peter 1:3-4.

27   Standing on the Promises of God: 2 Samuel 22:31c;

Job 2:10; 42:10-11; Psalm 18:30c; 27:13-14;
31:14-15; 91:14-16, NLT; Proverbs 3:5-6; Isaiah
26:3, NLT; Jeremiah 17:7; 29:11; John 16:33;
1 Thessalonians 5:18; Ephesians 5:20, NLT;
Habakkuk 2:4c; Romans 1:17c; Galatians 3:11b;
Hebrews 10:38a.

28   I Believe: 2 Samuel 22:31b; Psalm 18:30b;
Matthew 16:15-16; John 11:21-27; 14:2-3; Psalm
23:6b.

29   I Witness: Jeremiah 1:9; Matthew 10:19b-20, 27;
Acts 1:8, 4:29.

30   Please Pray for Me: Psalm 77:4b, NLT; Romans
8:26-27, 34.

31   Forgiven: Luke 12:47, NLT; Ephesians 2:10; James
4:17; 1 John 1:9.

32   Revelations: 2 Timothy 3:16-17, NLT; 2 Peter

1:20-21, NLT; Genesis 1:1, 26-28; John 1:1-3;
Colossians 1:15-22, NLT; 1 Corinthians 15:3-4;
John 1:12-13, NLT; Romans 8:16-17; Ephesians
1:4-5, NLT; 1 John 3:1, NLT; Ephesians 2:10, NLT;
2 Corinthians 4:14; 1 Peter 1:14-16, NLT; 2 Peter
3:10-13, NLT; Revelation 21:1-8, NLT.

33   Guilty As Charged: Matthew 22:35-38, NLT; John
      14:15, 21a, 23a, 24a, NLT; Matthew 25:31-46, NLT.

34   Remember This: 1 John 1:9; Isaiah 43:14a, 25, NLT;
      Jeremiah 31:34; Micah 7:18-19; Colossians 2:13;
      Isaiah 49:8a, 15d.

35   Lion on a Leash: Job 1:6-12; 2:1-7; Matthew
      26:41a; Mark 14:38a; Luke 22:31-32, 40b, 46b;
      John 14:30-31; 1 John 5:19; 1 Peter 5:8-9a; 2
      Peter 2:9, NLT; Psalm 31:1-8; 141:8-10.

36   Lesson Learned: Exodus 15:24; 16:2-3; Numbers
      11:1; 14:1-38; 21:4-6; 1 Corinthians 10:10-11;

Philippians 2:14; James 5:9, NLT; John 6:41-43; Ephesians 5:20; 1 Thessalonians 5:18; Psalm 30:12b; 136:1-9, NLT, 23-26, NLT.

37 Thank You, Father: John 10:10b, NKJV; 3:16; Psalm 107:1, 8, 15, 21, 31; refrain of Psalm 136:1-26; Jeremiah 31:3; Nehemiah 9:31; John 3:16; Acts 1:4-5; Psalm 118:24; Philippians 4:4.

38 You Know: Psalm 44:21, NLT; 69:5, NLT; 139:1-16, NLT; 1 Kings 8:39b, NLT; Matthew 6:32b, NLT; 10:30; Romans 5:8; 1 John 4:9-10.

39 Hound of Heaven: 1 Kings 8:23, MSG; Psalm 103:8; 2 Peter 3:9; 1 Timothy 1:15-16, NLT; 2:3b-4, NLT.

40 O God!: Psalm 22:2; 63:1; 69:1a, 3, NLT; 71:12.

41 Life Preserver: Psalm 18:2; 44:8, NLT; 69:16-17, 29; 70:1, 5; 71:12; 119:107, 145a, 147a, 149b, 154b, 159b, 170b, 175a; 143:7.

42   Solo Deo: Psalm 18:3a; 96:4-5; Romans 5:8;
      Philippians 2:5-11; 1 Peter 1:18-21, NLT; Revelation
      4:11; 5:9-13.

43   My Plea: Exodus 15:26b; 2 Kings 19:16a; Psalm
      4:3b; 5:2-3; 6:2; 6:9, NLT; 18:6; 28:2a; 30:2;
      41:4; 46:1; 54:2, NLT; 55:1-2a; 61:1; 69:3, NLT;
      70:1; 77:1; 84:8; 86:1; 88:9, NLT, 13; 102:1, 17;
      103:2-3; 121:2; 130:1, NLT; 141:1; 142:1, NLT;
      143:1, NLT.

44   A Repentant Sinner: Psalm 25:15; 31:4a; 40:3;
      51:1-2, 7, 9; 91:3a; 124:6a, 7; 141:8-9; John 8:36;
      1 John 1:9.

45   Rescue Me: Psalm 18:6; 28:2a, 6; 31:2, NLT, 5, NLT,
      9, NLT; 37:39-40, NLT; 40:2, NLT; 54:1a, NLT; 57:1a,
      2; 77:1-2; 86:3; 120:1; 130:1-2, NLT; 142:1, NLT.

46   My Helper: Numbers 11:4-13, 16a, 18-23,
      31-34; Joshua 10:12-14; 1 Samuel 1:1-20;

1 Kings 18:19-39; 2 Kings 20:1-7; 2 Chronicles
20:1-27; Psalm 27:9, NLT; 40:17b, NLT; 63:7, NLT;
118:7a; 121:2; Jonah 1:1-2:10; Matthew 8:1-3,
5-13; 9:18-25; 15:21-28; Mark 5:21-24, 35-42;
10:46-52; Acts 12:1-17; 16:22-34; Hebrews 13:6.

47   Promise Keeper: Exodus 34:5-6, NLT; Deuteronomy
7:9; Joshua 23:14b; Nehemiah 9:8b, NLT; Psalm
25:10, NLT; 100:5; 145:13, NLT; Lamentations
3:22-23, NLT; 2 Thessalonians 3:3.

48   An Appeal for Deliverance: Psalm 3:8a; 34:4;
40:17; 59:1; Matthew 5:44; 2 Corinthians 1:10;
2 Timothy 4:18, NLT.

49   Unconditional Surrender: Matthew 26:39, NLT; Luke
9:23; Romans 12:1, NLT; James 4:7a, 10; 1 Peter 5:6.

50   And the Blind Shall See: Psalm 146:8a; Mark
10:46-52; Luke 24:45; John 9:1-39; Hebrews
12:2a, NIV, 2b, NLT.

51   Honor Due: Exodus 20:12a; Isaiah 66:13a;
      Matthew 6:9; Romans 8:15, NLT; 2 Corinthians
      6:18, NLT; Ephesians 5:1, NLT; 6:2-3, NLT; Hebrews
      12:6-11, NLT; 1 John 3:1.

52   Celebrate Freedom: Psalm 118:5; Isaiah 61:1;
      Luke 4:18; John 8:36; Romans 6:6-7, NLT; 8:1-2;
      2 Corinthians 3:17; Galatians 5:1, NLT; 1 Timothy
      2:5-6a, NLT.

53   Prince of Peace: Isaiah 9:6; 26:3, NLT; 53:5; John
      16:33; Romans 5:1, NLT; Philippians 4:6-7, NLT.

54   Morning Joy: Psalm 5:3, NLT; 30:5b, NLT; 118:24;
      Lamentations 3:22-23, NLT; Mark 10:51; Acts 9:6,
      NKJV.

55   Evening Rest: Psalm 62:1a; 91:1, NLT; Matthew
      11:28.

56   A Christian's Creed: John 1:1-3, NLT; Colossians

1:15-17, NLT; Matthew 1:18-21, NLT; Luke 1:26-38,
NLT; John 6:35, NLT; Luke 2:1-7, NLT; Matthew
2:1-6; 11:2-5, NLT; 10:1, NLT; Isaiah 53:1-12, NLT;
Matthew 16:21; 17:22-23, NLT; 20:17-19, NLT;
26:14-28:10, 16-17; Mark 14:10-16:14; Luke
22:1-24:53; John 18:1-21:14; Romans 4:25;
1 Corinthians 15:3-8; Acts 1:3-11; Romans 8:34,
NLT; Matthew 24:29-31, NKJV; 1 Thessalonians
4:16-17; Revelation 7:9-17; 19:1-21:27.

57   I Love You, I Love You Not: Exodus 15:26, NLT;
2 Samuel 22:1-3, NLT; Psalm 3:3a, NLT; 7:10, NLT;
9:9, NLT; 18:1-2, NLT; 28:7a; 37:4, 39-40, NLT; 42:5,
11, NLT; 43:5, NLT; 70:5, NLT; 115:11, NLT; 116:1,
NLT; 118:7a; Isaiah 43:11, NLT; Habakkuk 3:19a;
Matthew 22:37-39; Luke 10:25-37; Romans 13:8,
NLT; 15:13, NLT; Ephesians 6:8, NLT; Colossians
3:24, NLT; Hebrews 11:6; 13:6; Revelation 22:12.

58   Help Wanted: 2 Corinthians 12:7-9; Philippians
4:11b-13; 2 Kings 2:9; 2 Peter 1:2, NLT.

59   Finisher of Our Faith: Philippians 1:6, NLT; John
      19:30; Hebrews 12:2, NKJV.

60   Effective Prayers: Romans 3:22-24, NLT; 4:21-25,
      NLT; Hebrews 4:16, NLT; Ephesians 3:12, NLT;
      Matthew 7:7-11, NLT; John 15:5-8, NLT; James
      5:16, NLT.

61   The Gift of Cancer: 2 Corinthians 12:7-9; Ephesians
      5:20, NLT; 1 Thessalonians 5:18.

62   My Creator and My Redeemer: Isaiah 43:1.

63   Prayer Warrior: Nehemiah 4:1-23; Psalm 27:14,
      NLT; 37:7a, NLT; 130:5-6a; Isaiah 8:17a; 40:31,
      NKJV; Ezekiel 3:17-19, NLT; 33:7-9, NLT; Matthew
      13:3-8, 18-23; Acts 8:1, 4, NLT; 1Corinthians 15:58,
      NLT; Galatians 6:9; Ephesians 6:7, NLT, 17, NLT;
      Colossians 3:23.

64   A Mind in Turmoil: Job 13:24, NLT; 19:11, NLT;

30:20a; 33:10; Psalm 2:4, NLT; 10:1, NLT; 13:1;
22:2, NLT; 33:10; 42:1-3, NLT; 44:23-24, NLT;
55:1-2, NLT; 77:1-2, NLT, 7-9, NLT; 88:1-14, NLT;
89:46-47a, NLT; Proverbs 13:12a.

65 Solace in Scripture: Psalm 42:5, 11, NLT; 43:5,
NLT; 107:19-20; 119:50, NKJV, 114, NLT; 130:5;
Romans 15:46, NLT; Philippians 4:6-7; 2 Timothy
3:16-17, NLT; 1 Peter 5:7.

66 Thank You, Jesus: Isaiah 53:3, NLT, 5, 10, NLT; John
3:16, NKJV.

67 Pro Bono: Psalm 9:1-2; 35:1-2, NLT, 9-11, NLT,
17-18, NLT, 23, NLT, 28, NLT; 100:4-5; 116:12, NLT,
17a, NLT; 118:1, 28-29; Jeremiah 51:36a, NLT;
Lamentations 3:58, NLT; 1 John 2:1, NLT.

68 To Do: James 4:7; 1 Peter 5:8-9; Matthew 5:44;
Luke 6:27, 35; Ephesians 4:32; Colossians
3:13; Matthew 6:14-15, NLT; Philippians 4:11b,

12; 1 Thessalonians 5:16-18; Philippians 4:4; Ephesians 5:20; 2:8-10.

69   My Weakness, Your Strength: Psalm 5:12; 28:7a; 30:5a; 46:1; 57:1-2; 84:11; 86:1, NLT, 3, NLT, 6, NLT, 16-17, NLT; 90:17; 106:4; 119:58, NKJV; Isaiah 41:10; John 15:5, NLT; Matthew 19:26; Philippians 4:13, NLT.

70   A Prayer for a Sick Friend: James 5:14-16, NLT.

71   Lord, Why Am I Suffering?: Leviticus 11:44-45; 19:2; 20:7-8; Deuteronomy 8:5, NLT; 31:8, NLT; Joshua 1:5b; Job 1:1-2:10; 13:15a; 36:21, NLT; Psalm 31:9-10; 32:1-5; 38:1-22; 39:9; 94:12; 102:1-11, NLT, 23-24, NLT; 118:5, NLT, 17-18, NLT; 119:67, 71, 92; Proverbs 3:11-12; Isaiah 38:10-17; 41:10; 43:2-3a, NLT; 48:10, NLT; Romans 5:3-4; 8:16-17, NLT; 8:28-29, NLT; 1 Corinthians 11:32; 2 Corinthians 1:3-4, 8-10, NLT; 4:8-9, NLT, 14, NLT, 16-18, NLT; 1 Thessalonians 3:2-4; 2 Timothy 3:12;

Hebrews 5:8, NLT; 12:6, NLT; James 1:2-4, 12,
NLT; 1 Peter 1:6-7, NLT, 15-16, NLT; 2:19-23, NLT;
3:14-18, NLT; 4:12-19, NLT.

72   Morning, Noon, and Night: Psalm 55:1-2, NLT,
      16-17, NLT, 22, NLT; 112:1, NLT, 4b, NLT, 7, NLT.

73   Total Commitment: Genesis 6:9-7:5; 12:1-5;
      22:1-18; Joshua 1:7-9; 3:9-17; 6:1-20; 1 Kings
      17:1-16; 2 Chronicles 20:1-30; Hosea 1:2-3, NLT;
      Jonah 3:1-4; Matthew 4:18-22; 16:24; Mark 14:32,
      35-36; Luke 24:44-46; John 14:15, 21a, 23; Acts
      8:26-40; 9:1-20; 10:1-48; 16:6-10; 18:9-11;
      26:9-20; 2 Corinthians 11:23-28; Hebrews 11:1-40.

74   Unspoken: Exodus 3:1-4:17; Judges 6:11-40;
      Romans 8:1; 2 Timothy 1:7.

75   To Be: Galatians 5:22-23a; Colossians 3:12-15.

76   Evening Star: Genesis 39:3, 23; Deuteronomy 8:18a,

NLT; Joshua 1:8; 14:6-14; 1 Samuel 18:14; Psalm
1:1-3, NLT; 22:9-10, NLT; 23:1-6; 28:7a; 34:15,
17; 37:4; 71:5-6, 9, 17-18, NLT; 92:12a, 14, NLT;
118:25b; 145:18-20a; Proverbs 3:5-6, NLT; 16:3;
Isaiah 41:10; 46:3b-4, NLT; Malachi 3:10; Matthew
6:33, NLT; John 10:11, 14-15; Philippians 4:13.

77   An Act of Faith: Deuteronomy 4:7b; Psalm 5:3, NLT;
17:6, NLT; 27:7; 28:1-2, NLT; 34:17, NLT; 63:1a,
4, NLT, 6, NLT; 66:16-20, NLT; 84:8; 88:13, NLT;
116:1-2, NLT, 10, NLT; 119:147a; 130:2; 141:1,
NLT; Proverbs 15:29, NLT; Jeremiah 29:12, NLT;
2 Corinthians 4:13, NLT; 1 Timothy 2:1-2, NLT, 8, NLT.

93   Acknowledgments: Deuteronomy 32:39, NLT;
Job 1:6-22; 2:1-10; 5:17-18; 42:10-11; Psalm
118:17-18, NLT; 119:67, 71, 75; Proverbs 3:11-12;
Hebrews 12:5-8, NLT; Isaiah 45:6-7; 53:10a;
1 Corinthians 11:32; 1 Peter 4:17, NLT; Revelation
3:19, NLT.

Acknowledgments

Thank you, LORD, for prompting me to write these prayer-poems. If you had not afflicted me, I would not — I could not — have written *A Pilgrim's Prayers*.

Thank you, Gail, for sharing your life and your love with me. Thank you for being my caregiver and my advocate when I was incapacitated.

Thanks to everyone who prayed for me.

Thanks to members of Camden Writers, the local chapter of South Carolina Writers Association, who've critiqued my manuscripts since 2007.

Thanks to the team at Courier Publishing — especially Butch Blume, who created the beautiful cover, and Denise Huffman, whose exquisite interior design transformed my manuscript into an attractive book.

Thanks to Lindsay Frost for the author's photograph.

Thank you, readers, for sharing this pilgrimage with me. I hope you're encouraged to pray frank, Scripture-based prayers whenever you go through daunting circumstances.

CPSIA information can be obtained
at www.ICGtesting.com
Printed in the USA
LVHW022106040821
693985LV00007B/28

9 781955 295000